Praise for Creating Calm

"Creating Calm is a great resource for not only kids but the parents too! It fosters an increase in self-awareness and provides the tools to help ease children's minds at night time when negative thoughts and emotions arise."
Courtney Hammer, ATR-BC, LPC, Art Therapist

"Meg's workbook is a great resource for children, parents, and teachers. This workbook provides practical ways to work through sleep anxieties and come up with tangible solutions. I highly recommend the book, I wish I had something like this for my students."
Grace Thomas, Elementary Teacher

Creating Calm

My Bedtime Workbook

Megan Menkis ATR-BC, LPC

Creating Calm

My Bedtime Workbook

Megan Menkis ATR-BC, LPC

MERAKI PRESS

PUBLISHING HOUSE

Additional copies may be purchased from Meraki Press.
Contact merakipress2021@gmail.com for information about bulk purchases or any other questions.

Cover Design: Megan Menkis
Illustrator: Megan Menkis
Layout Design: Katie Zeliger of Meraki Press

Printed in the U.S.A
First Edition: December 2023
ISBN: 979-8-218-08174-4

Megan Menkis ATR-BC, LPC
inspirecreativetherapy@gmail.com

Megan Menkis is a Licensed Professional Counselor and Board Certified Art Therapist. She has been practicing in PA for over 5 years and has a passion for working with children and families.

-For H.

NOW I LAY ME DOWN TO
SLEEP...
BUT WAIT!
I CAN'T SLEEP!

THERE'S JUST SO MUCH TO
THINK ABOUT. IT'S SO
DARK AND I FEEL SO
ALONE AND THERE ARE
TOO MANY THINGS TO BE
AFRAID OF!

If you've ever felt like this, then this book is for you!

The pages in this book have different ideas that can help you feel calm enough to fall asleep. After you are done with the whole book, re-read it at night with your adult to help you remember what you've learned.

There are a lot of reasons it can be hard to fall asleep at night.

Maybe your brain won't stop thinking.

Or your body won't stop moving.

Or your bed is uncomfortable.

Or you are nervous for what's happening the next day.

Or there's just too much to feel scared about!

Why is it hard for you to fall asleep at night?

_____

_____

_____

_____

_____

Did you know...

What you think about at night time can make it harder for you to fall asleep. When you think about calm things, your brain and body feel calm.

If you think about scary things at night, your brain and body can feel scared.

What is Mindfulness?

Mindfulness is when you pay attention to your thoughts and how they make you feel.

Being mindful can help calm your mind and body and help you sleep at night.

It takes a lot of practice to be mindful. You can try it on the next few pages!

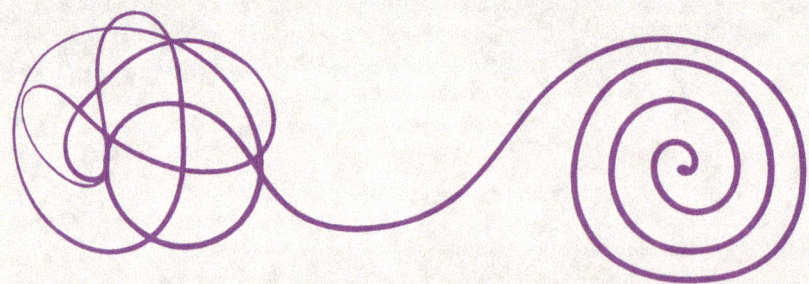

What thoughts keep you awake at night?

(write or draw them below)

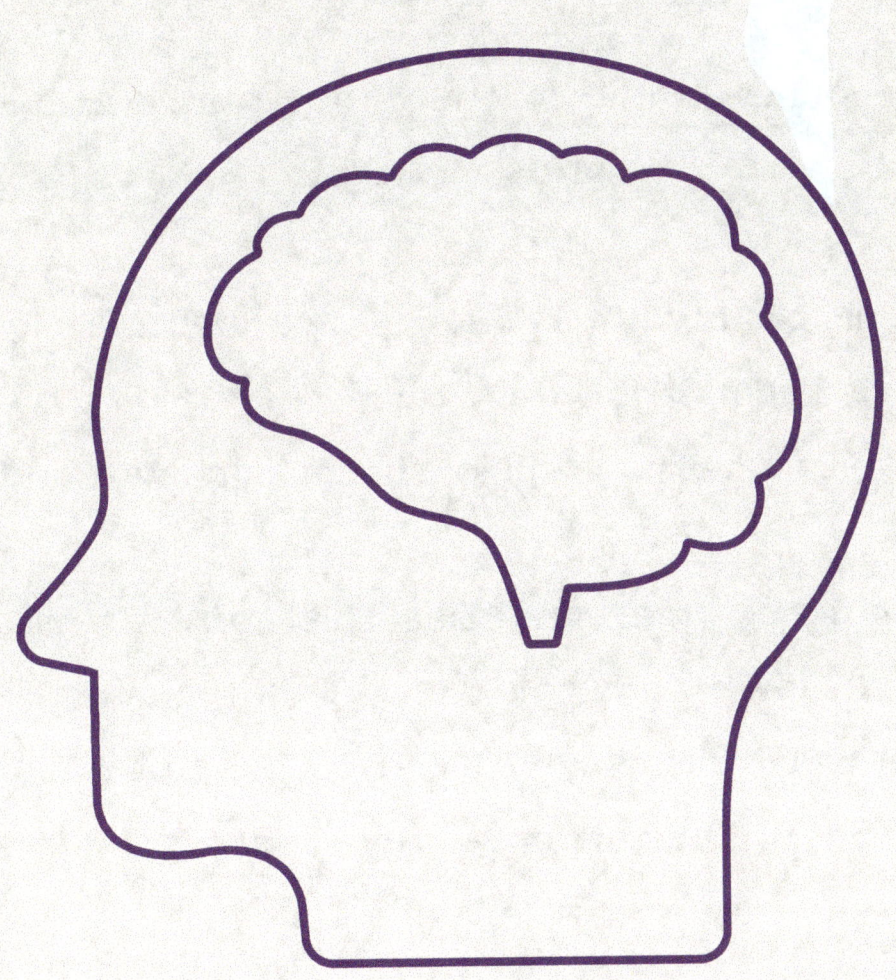

Practicing Mindfulness

Have you ever laid in the grass and watched the clouds float by?

Imagine that your thoughts are like the clouds. You see them, and you watch them float by. You don't focus on any of them for too long.

On the next page, practice this for **2-3** minutes. Write down some of the thought clouds that float by. Were any hard to let float by? Which ones, and why?

My Thought Clouds

Cloudy Thoughts vs. Sunny Thoughts

Sometimes your thoughts can get stuck in your brain. It can make your mind feel cloudy, and it can be hard to think about other things.

When this happens, you can try to remember more happy, sunny thoughts.

On the next page, write down some of the "cloudy" thoughts that get stuck in your mind, and then write a different "sunny thought." Look at the example, or have your adult help you come up with ideas.

Cloudy Thoughts vs. Sunny Thoughts

What if something bad happens?

I am safe. I am strong and brave.

_____

_____

_____

_____

_____

_____

_____

_____

_____

_____

_____

_____

_____

_____

Here's how I feel at night:

(circle all that apply)

Angry

Worried

Scared

Tired

Alone

Sad

Restless

Calm

Excited

This is how I feel in my body when I can't sleep:

(circle all that apply)

Heart Pounding

Tight Muscles

Trouble Breathing

Hot and Sweaty

Crying

Screaming

Hiding

Did you know...

Taking big, deep breaths before bed time can help calm your mind and your body.

Try breathing in and out so your belly moves up and down. This gets the most air to your brain to help it relax.

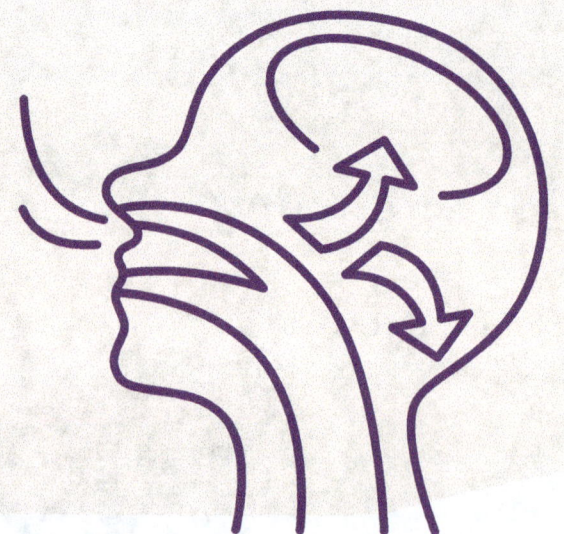

Deep Breathing

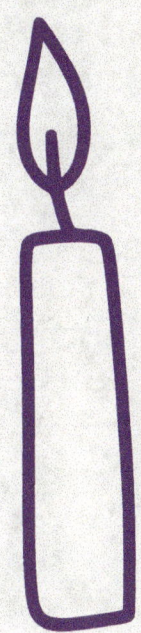

Breath in

through your nose

like you are smelling a flower

Breath out

through your mouth

like you are blowing out a candle

Remember....

It takes practice to stay calm and mindful. Try not to be upset if it doesn't work the first time.

It's like learning to ride a bike. The more you practice, the better you get!

Activity:
Progressive Muscle Relaxation

What is progressive muscle relaxation? (PMR)
You can help your body relax by making different muscles really tight and tense, and then relaxing them. Try squeezing your fists together now and holding it while you count to 10, then relax. Do your hands feel any different?

Your body and your brain are connected, and when you calm your body, your brain calms down too.

Try it out and then tell your adult how it feels!

Find a cozy spot to sit or lie down
Breathe in and tighten your muscles
Hold for 10 seconds
Breathe out and relax your muscles
Gradually work your way through your different muscle groups
(ideas on next page)

Activity:

Progressive Muscle Relaxation

Pretend you are squeezing a lemon in your hands, under your arms, or between your knees.

Pretend you are a cat who is waking up from a nap, and stretch your arms out as far as you can. Then stretch out your legs.

Pretend you are a turtle going in and out of your shell. Bring your shoulders up to your ears, hold, and then release.

Pretend a fly landed on your nose. Wiggle it off by scrunching your face.

*Tip: There are lots of PMR videos for kids on youtube, just search "Progressive Muscle Relaxation for Kids"

Activity:

Progressive Muscle Relaxation

Activity:
Progressive Muscle Relaxation

Add your own idea!
Draw a picture to show a way
you can tighten and then relax your muscles.

Activity:
Worry Box

Supplies needed:
Old tissue box or cardboard box
Markers
Stickers, Craft Supplies, Glue, Paper

Directions:
Use craft supplies to decorate your box. This will be your very own "worry box" to keep by your bed. Before going to sleep, write down any worries, fears, or scary thoughts you have and place them in the box.
After writing down your thoughts, try to let them go. You can imagine that the box is a friendly monster gobbling up your worries, or a safe spot to hold on to them and talk about them with an adult later.

It can be helpful to think of a happy phrase to repeat to yourself when you have trouble sleeping at night.

I am safe.

I am loved.

I will have good dreams.

Add your own:

_____

Or, you can think about the good things that happened today, or the things you are grateful for

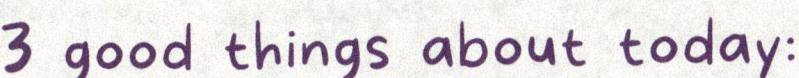

3 good things about today:

_____

_____

_____

3 Things I am Grateful For
(draw or write in the boxes below)

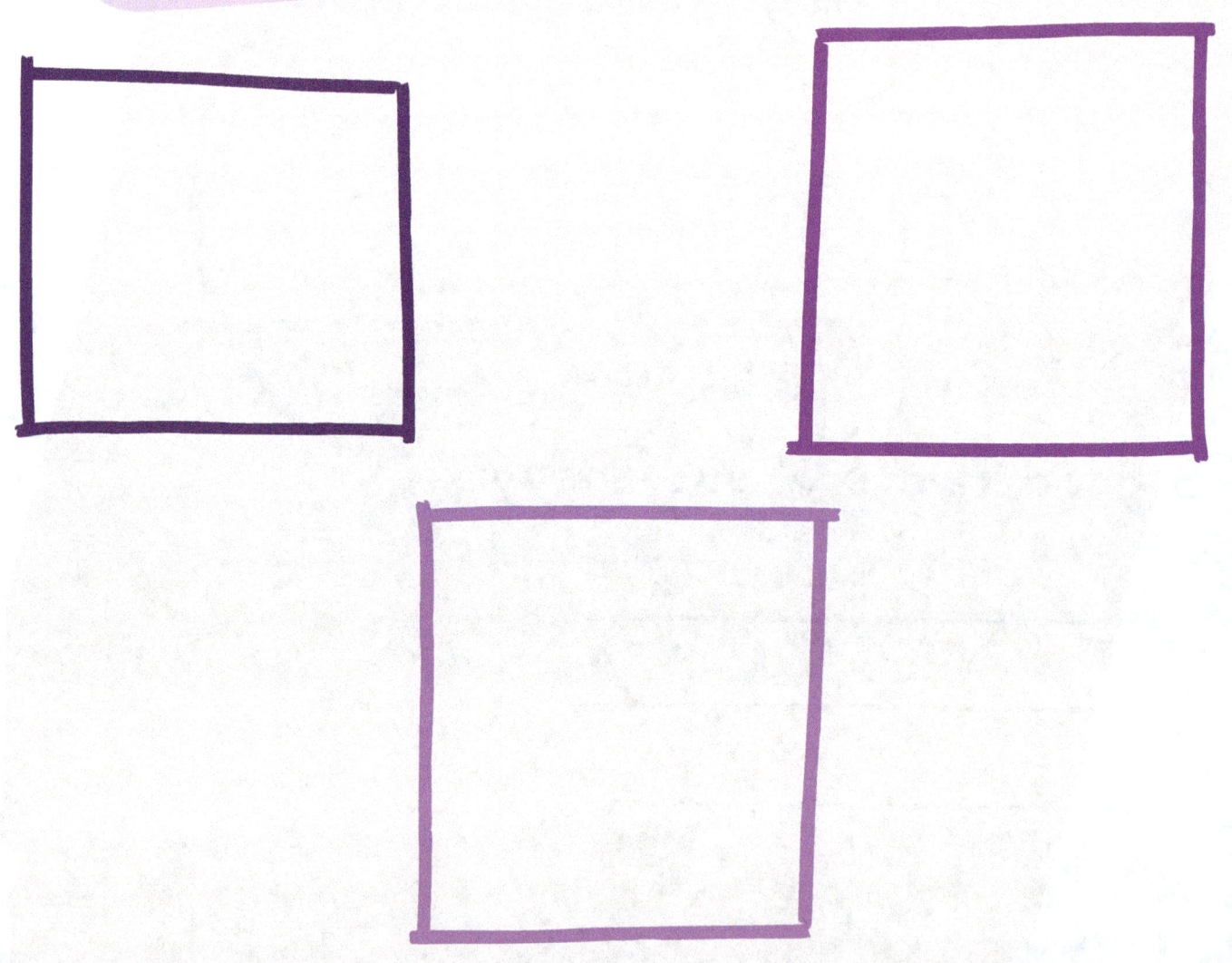

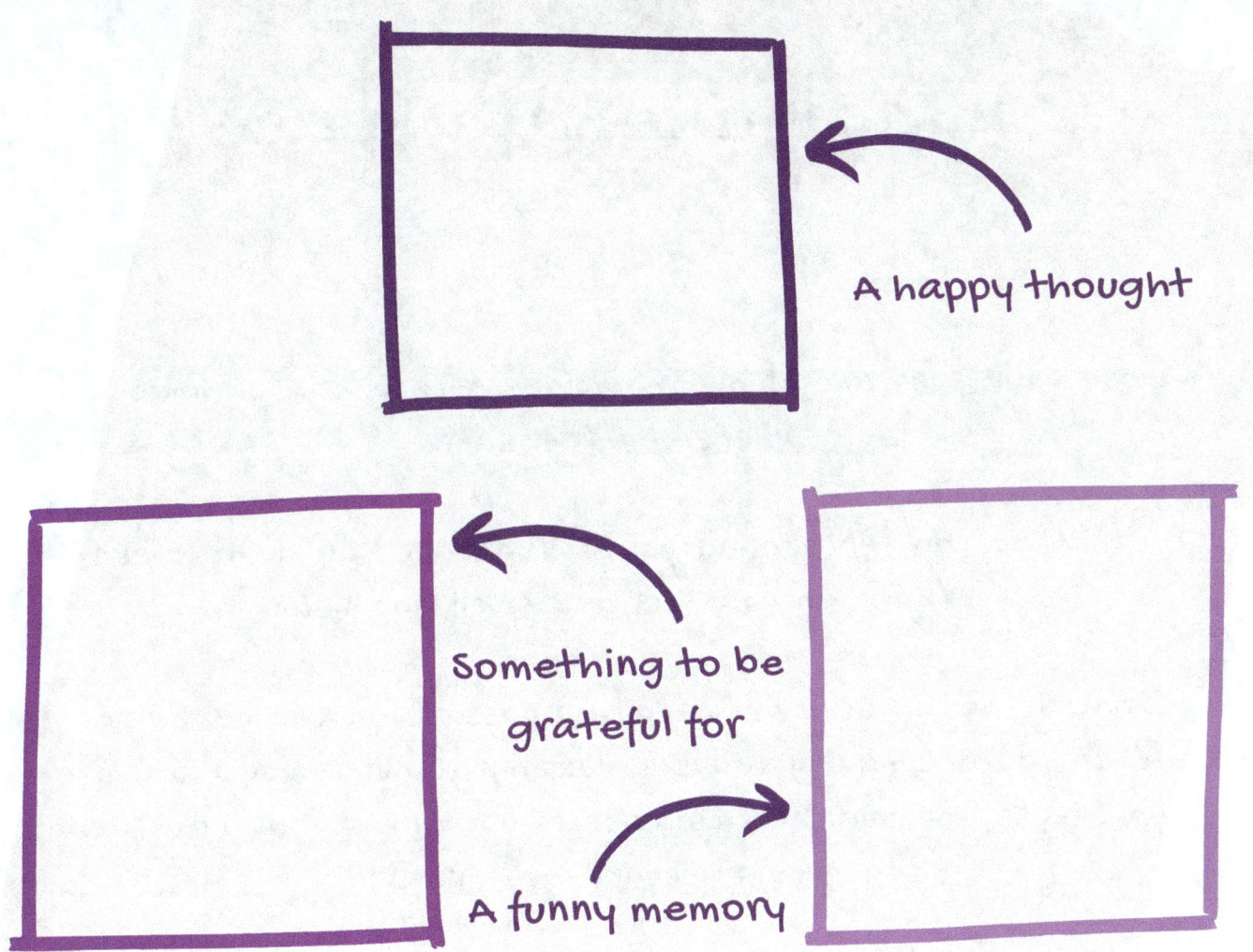

A happy thought

Something to be grateful for

A funny memory

Let's Review!

Write or draw some examples of positive thoughts. You can think about these things when you are trying to fall asleep.

Imagine a Safe Space

Close your eyes and think of a place, either real or imagined, where you feel safe.

What do you see around you? What are you doing there? What can you feel and smell and hear?

Draw it out in as much detail as possible on the next page. When you are having trouble sleeping at night, you can close your eyes and imagine this place in your mind. You can even hang your picture by your bed!

My Safe Space

Calm, Quiet, Peaceful

What do the words calm, quiet, and peaceful mean to you? You want your body and brain to feel this way at night so that it is easier to get to sleep.

Think of pictures to match the words Calm, Quiet, and Peaceful. Try to think of something different for each one, and draw it on the next page.

Calm, Quiet, Peaceful

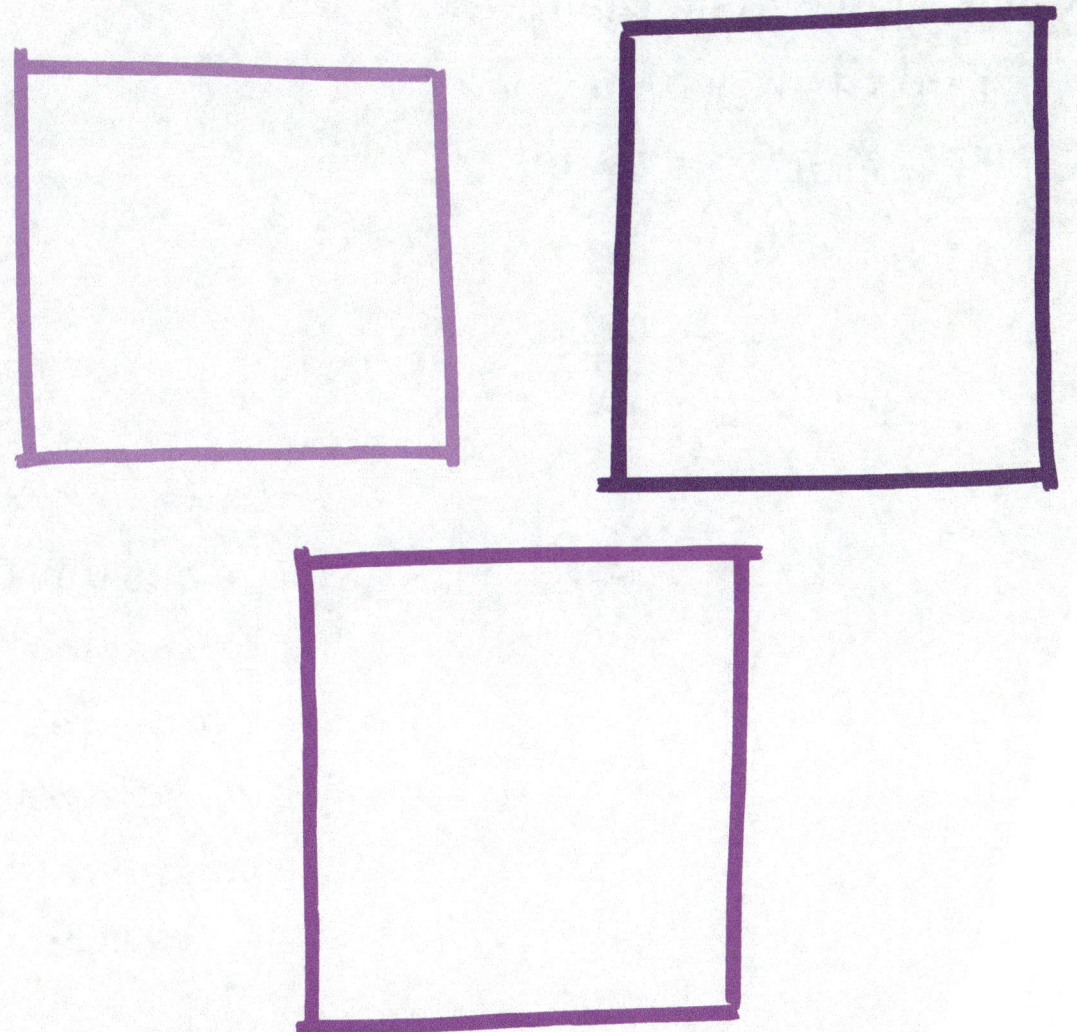

Did you know...

Making your room feel safe at night can help you relax and get better sleep.

The next few pages will focus on making your room feel as safe and comfortable as possible.

Things I already have in my room that make me feel safe:

Get Creative!

Draw your dream room:

What I can add to my room to feel safe and comfortable at night:

Talk it out with your adult, and see if any of these ideas are doable! Here are some ideas from other kids:

Play calming music or white noise

Try a weighted blanket

Keep the door open

Add an extra night light

Add a nice smell, like lavender spray

Activity:

Sweet Dreams Pillow Case

Supplies needed:
White Pillow Case
Fabric Markers

Directions:
Think of all the positive memories and happy things you want to dream about, and draw or write them on your pillow case with the fabric markers. When you put your head on your pillow at night, you can use these pictures to help you focus on happy thoughts. Maybe you will even dream about them!

Activity:

Sleep Music or Sleep Stories

Supplies needed:
Speaker
Calming Music
Relaxing Story

Directions:
Listening to something calming can help your brain relax at night. You can try instrumental music or an audio book. If you don't know where to start, you can ask your adult to search "Kid's Sleep Stories" on youtube. These videos can help you practice relaxing your muscles and brain, while also telling a story!

Activity:

Sleep Music or Sleep Stories

A list of music and stories
that are calming to me:

_____

_____

_____

_____

_____

Activity:
Turn Your Fears into Funnies

If you think about scary things at night, try turning your fear into something silly. If you are afraid of monsters under the bed, imagine that they are there to tell you jokes! If you keep thinking about that spelling test tomorrow, pretend that your teacher reads the words using a silly voice!

Try it out on the next page. Imagine turning your fear into the silliest thing you can think of!

Draw your fear as something silly, and then tell a story about it

My Funny Fear

Did you know...

It is important to have a bedtime routine that helps you feel calm. This means you do the same, or similar things each night before bedtime. Here is one example...

Put PJ's on
Brush Teeth
Read books
Sing a song
Hugs and Kisses

Talk to your adult about what would help you feel most calm at night, and create your own night time routine.

_____

_____

_____

_____

_____

Tips for Success: Focus on calming, relaxing things. Try to stay away from scary stories or the bright light of the TV about an hour before bedtime.

Congratulations!

You completed the workbook!
Remember to keep practicing what you learned.

Let's Review:

2 things I learned:

_____

_____

What was most helpful:

_____

Something I want to keep working on:

_____

Information for Parents and Caregivers

Here are some helpful practices to encourage relaxation and good sleep:
(This is also called "Sleep Hygiene")

Bedtime Routines
Regular sleep and wake times
Check noise and light levels in the room
No screens 1 hour before bed time
Avoid Caffeine
Don't eat right before bed time
Get lots of natural light during the day.

Information for Parents and Caregivers

When your kid isn't sleeping, you're not sleeping....
We get it, you're exhausted too!

Remember, if you occasionally need to let your child climb in bed with you so you can get some sleep, that is OK!

Getting your child to develop healthy sleep habits is a process that requires patience.

Supporting an Anxious Child at Bedtime

If there is a quick, easy answer to your child's worry, you can try to deal with it right away.

Otherwise, you can make a plan to deal with the worry at a later time (try using the worry box!) and encourage your child to focus on something else.

Remember to validate your child's feelings.

"I understand you're worried about X, let's talk about it tomorrow.

Right now, let's focus on 3 things we are grateful for today."

Supporting an
Anxious Child at Bedtime

Remind your child you are here to talk and help them work through their feelings, but try not to go into "fix it" mode too quickly. Remember, reassurance usually only gives more power to children's worries and teaches them to rely on you.

Instead, try to gently guide your child to come up with their own solution. Get curious and ask questions such as "I wonder what you think would help?"

What about Nightmares?

Nightmares and Night Waking are common, especially during times of transition in your child's life.

You can give your child a security object to comfort them (a blanket, stuffed animal, or maybe even your shirt!)

Leave a dim light on

Leave the door cracked open

Use a baby monitor or walkie-talkies to keep the line of communication open at night

What about Nightmares?

Use your child's imagination to try to help them process their scary thoughts or bad dreams.

Have them draw a picture of their dream, then rip it up or throw it away to banish the dream.

In the morning, talk about a different ending the dream could have - is it a happy or silly ending?

Label a spray bottle as "anti-monster" potion and spray it in your child's room before bed.

More Resources

If your child's sleep is affecting their mood, relationships, or behavior - don't hesitate to reach out to your pediatrician for more ideas.

You can find more information on Sleep Hygiene and Healthy Sleep Habits on the Center for Disease Control or American Academy of Pediatrics websites.

For more information on supporting your Anxious Child, visit Child Mind Institute at https://childmind.org/article/what-to-do-and-not-do-when-children-are-anxious/

About the Author

Megan Menkis is a Licensed Professional
Counselor and Board Certified Art
Therapist. She has been practicing in PA
for over 5 years and has a passion for
working with children and families.

Check out her other Books:

Super Ears: My Misophonia Workbook

Spectacular Senses: My Sensory Processing
Workbook

www.ingramcontent.com/pod-product-compliance
Lightning Source LLC
Chambersburg PA
CBHW080856120626
46553CB00009B/2645